ABANDONED COAL TOWNS
—— OF ——
SOUTHERN WEST VIRGINIA

MICHAEL JUSTICE

AMERICA
THROUGH TIME®
ADDING COLOR TO AMERICAN HISTORY

America Through Time is an imprint of Fonthill Media LLC
www.through-time.com
office@through-time.com

Published by Arcadia Publishing by arrangement with Fonthill Media LLC
For all general information, please contact Arcadia Publishing:
Telephone: 843-853-2070
Fax: 843-853-0044
E-mail: sales@arcadiapublishing.com
For customer service and orders:
Toll-Free 1-888-313-2665

www.arcadiapublishing.com

First published 2021

ISBN 978-1-63499-310-4

Typeset in Trade Gothic 10pt on 15pt
Printed and bound in England

Contents

About the Author

Michael Justice is a photography enthusiast who enjoys urban exploration, most things odd and peculiar. He is from West Virginia and currently resides in East Tennessee. He has a passion for art and storytelling through photography.

Introduction

This book is a collection of images from abandoned or forgotten coal towns and their surrounding areas in West Virginia's southern coal fields. This is not an exhaustive collection; it is just the beginning of what will be a continued journey through the state and those bordering it to document and preserve history through photography. You will not find specific details about any of the locations of the buildings throughout this collection. This is intentional and done as an effort to help protect the buildings from vandals and further destruction. The mountains of West Virginia are home to numerous scenic wonders. This is not a representation of the beauty of the state, but a documentation of what happens when we forget and Mother Nature takes over. Beneath the vines and dirt lay decades of history waiting to be discovered, and I welcome you on this photographic journey with me. Through the images in this book, you will get an up-close view of the texture, grit, and mood of these amazing structures. While they may appear tattered and torn, there's a silent beauty to be found within the walls of each structure. I hope you enjoy the images and may you be inspired to take a few backroads on your next trip and appreciate the beauty of forgotten America.

1

The Powerhouse

This powerhouse was built by the Pocahontas Coal Company in the early 1900s and supplied electricity to several area mining operations for many years. This spectacular operation was shut down as the coal companies started their exit many years ago. It sits towering over the community, tucked away in the heart of the Appalachian Mountains. You can't help but be amazed by the size of this building as you turn the corner and see it for the first time sitting on top of the hill. I can only imagine how busy this place once was, as you can see the expansive workspace on each level. There's still so much potential in a location of this size. If it wasn't located in such a remote part of the state, I could easily see it being repurposed for an elaborate hotel. With an excellent view of the tracks, it would be a must-see destination for train lovers. However, for now we can at least appreciate the building for what it is and the decaying beauty it holds inside. Oh, and maybe forget about any unaccounted footsteps or whistling that you might encounter, as I'm sure there's a lot of that as well.

Welcome to the powerhouse.
Isn't this view amazing?

Let's take a tour of this open concept workspace.

Have a seat. No, wait—that's just a wooden frame and a door.

Danger! Who doesn't love abandoned chemicals.

This must be for those potentially exploding chemical bottles.

Below: At this doorway and connecting room, I had two strange experiences. Maybe I wasn't really alone in this big building.

Wouldn't this make a lovely wedding venue.

The third level houses more electrical equipment in these locker-style boxes. It also allows you to get a good view if you look over the railing. There are still no signs of those random footsteps from earlier.

Below: There's a lot going on in this picture. This work desk is surrounded by the equipment used to keep the station operational. There's a large switchboard in the back and some shelving units on the right. The lights also have the old-style globes still intact. Kuddos to all the random guests for not smashing all the glass in here.

Above: This is where it gets fun. Above those radiators are two guard pigeons, or that is what I choose to believe they are after almost giving me a heart attack.

2

Coal Company Store and Office #1

The state has many wonderful coal company stores, and they were once the only way for their employees to spend the company money. This location is one of many that I will document throughout this book; it is the largest I have visited in the state as well. There were once efforts to restore many of these company stores, but time has not been kind to these once bustling businesses. While the largest, this location is also the best preserved of all the stores I have visited. It is registered on the national register of historic places and has some interesting history, as most in this part of the state were all designed by the same architect. This building is not in complete disrepair but has suffered fire damage and what appears to be some uninvited guests contributing to the damage and creepiness of the building. A bassinet and stroller are a few of the last things you hope to find in an abandoned building. I could fill an entire book with the treasures in this location, and who knows? One day I might. Let's take a quick look at this elaborate multi-building, multi-floor piece of West Virginia history.

Above: The front of this massive building from across the street showing two wings and the covered walkway between them. This is the only company store I've seen with this much detail placed into the stone work and design of layout.

Left: There's a beautiful stone walkway between the buildings. It's in excellent shape and provides a nice view of the courtyard.

Hey, there's a yard sale going on here in the courtyard, who would've known. Anyone need a bassinet?

As if seeing the bassinet wasn't creepy enough, as I enter one of the buildings, I find the deeply discounted stroller laying in the corner. It may just be me, but nothing is creepier than seeing items for a child in a completely abandoned place.

Let us pull up a chair and enjoy the cozy surroundings in this dark and dusty company store. Looks like a great place to grab some coffee. Surprisingly, I did not see a mattress in this building.

This room has clearly seen better days. The tarp on the floor beckons a kill room vibe with its somehow dirt floor on a concrete foundation and broken shelves and items in the background. Even the wall has been busted open to reveal what appeared to be a very dark storage area. This could've been where the mattress was hiding as I didn't go very far into this room.

Here's a nicely decorated hallway with peeling paint and crumbling ceilings. There's so much texture in these places. I quickly put on a mask to breathe through, just to be safe.

Above: I saw a random room off to the side that had this large wooden box in the center of the room. I'm sure it's haunted or home to something that goes bump in the night.

Right: Yes, this is a sink in the hallway. This place literally has it all. It's almost move-in ready. It just needs a little TLC, so make your offers now.

3

The Fuel Company Store and Office Building

Southern West Virginia is not without its share of abandoned coal company stores. This location has two buildings across the street from one another, making the drive out a little more worth the trip. One served as the company store and the other as the offices. There's little left to tell them apart and they share the same architect as the others listed in this collection. These buildings are not as intricate and follow more of the box style with two levels. The second floor in both buildings were inaccessible due to years of neglect. Nothing inside the buildings would give an indication of a storefront or the post office that was once housed inside them. Instead, you'll find graffiti, a filthy mattress, trash, and beer bottles—you know, the typical décor of an abandoned building. At least we have some inspirational graffiti inside, which is a welcomed sight in my opinion. There's also what I am calling the secret window with a view of nature. Enjoy your quick trip around these two locations and hopefully you stay dry, as it was raining on me.

Exterior for Building number 1 which has the most interesting items I captured.

Exterior for Building number 2 which was basically a large box and stripped of everything inside.

Inside you can see an open space with graffiti on almost every wall. The elevators have long been removed or destroyed and there are no signs of steps to gain access to the second level. The ceilings have all fallen out and crunches beneath your feet. There was access to the basement in this building, but there wasn't any lighting and the steps appeared to be gone, so I did not venture there, as I was alone.

Inside building number 1 we find a lot more rooms. In the front room you can see a long hallway that leads to the back and where the steps to the second level once were.

I wanted to go up to the second level but the steps have literally been removed from this building. You can see the opening to the basement, but I wasn't heading down there on this lonely rainy day.

This is the secret window. I have no clue what this small room would've been or why it needed a window, but I loved the light and composition it provided in the darkness near the back.

If you look a little closer, you'll find boxed springs and a mattress. It's as if they were expecting me and wanted to make it feel a little welcoming. I wasn't so sure about the clown faces on the wall, so I passed on spending the night.

4

Coal Company Store #2

This is another coal company store by the same architect. It has one large building on the site and several wings off the main building. I spent a lot of time roaming around this building as it twisted and turned with a basement and two floors. This building was fantastic to visit; you can imagine just how grand this once was. The building appeared to have been cleaned out once, but a fire and subsequent water damage from years exposed to the weather has made it less likely to be restored. It is also on the national registry for historic places and served as the focal point for the community in its heyday. I can say that I wouldn't have been surprised to be greeted by someone around one of the corners, as it has signs of recent visitors.

A common theme among these coal company stores is abandoned furniture. While I love the aesthetics they provide, they make one extra cautious when rounding a dark corner. Tip: don't get caught on the other side of the tracks, as the train may decide to stop for whatever reason, leaving you no choice but to stick around a little longer than planned. This building was one of the seedier locations on this list that I visited. I had to watch every step to make sure I stayed safe. Pull up a seat on the sofa where it's a little safer and allow me to be your personal tour guide of this historic landmark.

Here we find a nice futon for those in the market or maybe you need to rest after taking a few stairs into this water filled company store.

This room screams, "Nope!"

Above: The sun roof is a nice touch to this crumbling little gem of a room.

Right: This corridor reminds me of something from a dream sequence in a nightmare. You've got the ceiling peeling off, a dark doorway, and an unwelcoming forest outside.

I don't know why, but I find the graffiti in here a little comical. Maybe it's because the horned figure is smiling at me.

This is the second level; the steps were covered in about a foot of sediment. You can see some of that at the base of the doorway into the room.

5

Thurmond

Thurmond is now a ghost town but was once a thriving coal town located on the New River. This location is well known and has some amazing views of the river. If you stop on the drive down, you can take in the views of some of the small waterfalls created by the river. While Thurmond is a ghost town, the train tracks are still active, so you can visit the abandoned town and take in some train watching while you are there. The main tracks are what everyone tends to visit, as you can see the tipple with the post office and old buildings lining main street. However, if you continue to the end and take the high road, you can take in a better view and see a few more abandoned houses along the top road.

The church is also along the backroad. If you are into ghost towns, railroads, or Westerns, this is a place to visit. I made this trip on a very hot July day, so pay attention to the weather forecast, bring lots of water, and dress appropriately, as there is little shade while roaming around.

Welcome to Thurmond, tucked away in the mountains and past small waterfalls and some of the best white-water rafting you'll find.

This is the booming downtown area of Thurmond, where some internet searches suggest was once the longest running poker game.

This is the coal tipple standing in the heart of Thurmond.

Under the tipple you could explore the loading tracks if you were brave enough. The wood has seen better days, and if you lost your footing in this area you were sure to fall in a hole and break a few bones.

The only way in or out of Thurmond is across a single-lane bridge with the tracks right next to it.

I didn't realize the tracks were active until I saw trains passing through so be careful when exploring.

The sign says it all and was probably my favorite picture from Thurmond. Someone needs to film a Zombie Western at this location.

6

Nuttallburg Coal Mining Complex

Nuttallburg is another (more well-known) coal complex that receives visitors, as it is located close to white water rafting and camping attractions in the New River area. This is definitively worth the detour if you find yourself in the area. It has one of the most complete coal tipples that I've been able to visit and would make for a good time during any season.

Nuttallburg mining camp sits along the New River, and during its operation was once leased by Henry Ford. The Nuttallburg mining complex is off the beaten path, but it is a nice scenic drive to relax and take in some nature and views of the New River Gorge area. As you can see in the following images, there's a complete tipple with tracks below, along with some mining equipment. If you travel down the path a little longer, you will come to the remnants of the coke oven and company store located in the woods.

When you walk up, you see the coal tipple intact with the mining conveyor running from the mines on the mountain down to the tracks near the river where the coal was loaded and transported out. Or you can pretend this is a Walker from the *Star Wars* movies.

You can walk under the loading tower on the partial tracks to get a good view of how they would operate the machinery.

As you look around you'll see discarded machinery and scraps of twisted metal rusting away.

Be careful getting too close to the broken down and rusted equipment, it's a long drive back out to get a tetanus shot.

If you venture down the trail, you'll come across the ruins of the coke ovens used at Nuttallburg.

At the end of the trial are the remnants of the company store that served the mining camp.

7

Coal and Coke Company Offices plus Community Pool

The office was once the central headquarters for the U.S. coal efforts in the area. It was the heart of the coal camp in this town and operated until the 1970s. It has since suffered flood and fire damage, making it a little less than desirable. The neighbors are really friendly; they will make sure to let you know that it's not safe to enter. The weeds have overgrown the sidewalk in front, so it's hard to see that sections are missing, and you can easily break a leg before getting close enough to find a way in. With all the warnings, I admired this building from a distance and then moved on to some locations down the street.

The pool and stadium are just around the corner and up the hill on the way to grandmother's house. Well, maybe not exactly—but it is very close and pool was operational for a lot longer than the coal company offices. The stadium has served as fair grounds in the past and an observation area for the annual Independence Day fireworks display. I'm not so certain they are used for much now and I don't think anyone is working the lifeguard station at the pool either.

Come take a swim at the local pool. This was still operational when I was a child but had been empty for a while now.

8

Mining Company Workshop and School

This is the mining town of the famed Rocket Boys. I could stop there, as the books, movies, and internet have documented this area far greater than myself. What I am going to show you is one of the remaining mining company workshops and the old school. A workshop like this would've been where the boys had help building their first rockets, turning those early dreams into a reality. This mining operation remained open until the 1980s and was once one of the largest mining operations in the state. The workshop depicted here is one of the only remaining structures from this mining company but has one of my favorite pictures and personal stories. On this same site they once had stores, housing, offices, and a public pool. Some of these are still standing but are not shown in this collection. Last, you will see images of the old school, which has suffered severe damage from a fire. Most of the interior rooms are no longer standing, and Mother Nature has taken advantage of there being no roof, with mature trees now replacing what would be classrooms, gyms, and cafeterias. This location has been captured by almost anyone wanting to visit the famed sites of southern West Virginia, so I hope you enjoy my creative take on this abandoned location.

I love all the windows and while some are busted, there's still a lot of glass remaining that makes for great pictures.

Come get your hot dogs! This is one of the most random finds in an abandoned mining facility that I've come across.

Looking through the back you can see the workshop extends and has more work space. The lights are still hanging, and it shelters a tractor near the doorway.

Just down the road is the old high school. It's seen better days for sure, but this entrance is still spectacularly welcoming in an apocalyptic kind of way.

Once inside, you will see the remnants of the inner workings of the school but not much else. Nature has started to reclaim this building and the top floor has trees growing from the hallway.

9

Miscellaneous:
Hidden Treasures on the Road to the Prize

The following images were taken in or around one of the coal towns while traveling backroads during what sometimes is just a desire to take the long way to my destination. I always keep an eye out for abandoned houses, rusted vehicles, or run-down signs that will make for an interesting image. Sometimes, these one-off images are my favorite parts of the entire trip. They are sometimes the only images I get, as the main location was either demolished or not accessible, so they help me keep my sanity. This odd collection is also sort of how I started this hobby anyway, so it's only fitting to end with them.

All images were taken while traveling backroads and detours in southern West Virginia. Some I happened to find while looking for blackberries with family when visiting, and others I just got lucky to see. Enjoy these hidden treasures, as without this section, they would forever be bound to my Instagram account or left on my computer to fade into history, as many of these places soon will do.

This was once a beautiful house in a sleepy coal town. I remember going by here on my way to visit friends.

Who doesn't like a funeral home? This is what's left after some major floods.

Final Note

I hope that you've enjoyed this photographic journey into a few of the hidden gems southern West Virginia has to offer. I would also like to thank you for your curiosity and support of America Through Time's abandoned series. I look forward to sharing my next journey with you very soon. I would also like to thank the people who made this possible. First, my wife, whose support in my weird hobbies is unequivocal. I would also like to thank Toddzilla and Big Red for your support and allowing me to drag you along on some of my adventures. Finally, I would like to thank my trusty cats, who sit with me while I filter through pictures late at night editing; I will blame their cat antics for any typos in this book.